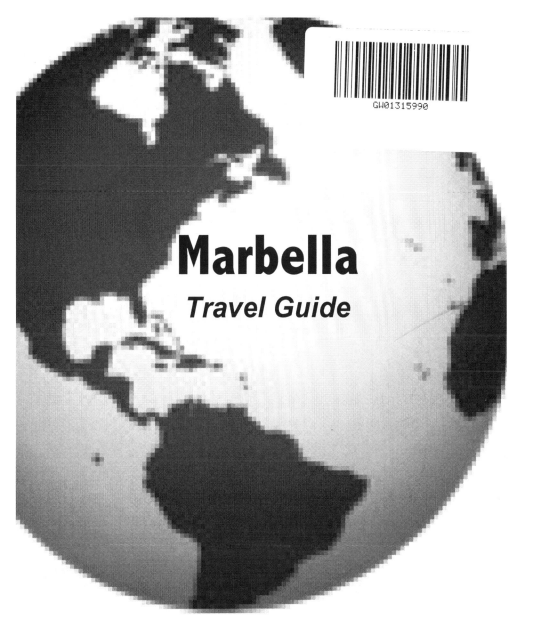

Marbella
Travel Guide

Quick Trips Series

No part of this publication may be reproduced, stored in a retrieval system, or transmitted, in any form or by any means without the prior written permission of the publisher, nor be otherwise circulated in any form of binding or cover other than that in which it is published and without similar condition being imposed on the subsequent purchaser. If there are any errors or omissions in copyright acknowledgements the publisher will be pleased to insert the appropriate acknowledgement in any subsequent printing of this publication. Although we have taken all reasonable care in researching this book we make no warranty about the accuracy or completeness of its content and disclaim all liability arising from its use.

Copyright © 2016, Astute Press
All Rights Reserved.

Table of Contents

MARBELLA — 6
- 🌐 PLANNING YOUR STAY 10
- 🌐 CLIMATE & WEATHER 12

SIGHTSEEING — 15
- 🌐 SELWO ADVENTURE SAFARI PARK 15
- 🌐 MUSEUM OF CONTEMPORARY SPANISH ENGRAVING 17
- 🌐 PUERTO BANÚS & MARINA 19
- 🌐 JÚZCAR SMURF VILLAGE 21
- 🌐 MARBELLA OLD TOWN & ORANGE TREE SQUARE 23
- 🌐 CHURCH OF OUR LADY 24
- 🌐 RONDA & TAJO GORGE 25
    - Tajo Gorge 27
- 🌐 GRAZALEMA & UBRIQUE VILLAGES 28
    - Grazalema 29
    - Ubrique 30
- 🌐 CONSTITUTION PARK 32
- 🌐 BONSAI MUSEUM 33
- 🌐 HORSE & CARRIAGE TOUR 34
- 🌐 ESTEPONA 35
    - Museums of Palaeontology, Ethnography, Bullfighting, Image & Sound 38
    - Parque San Isidro & Necropolis Visitor Centre 39
- 🌐 FUNNY BEACH AMUSEMENT PARK 40
- 🌐 BOAT TRIPS FROM MARBELLA TO PUERTO BANUS 42

🌐 Alcornocales Natural Park & Cortes de la Frontera 43
🌐 Golf Courses 45
Los Naranjos 46
Marbella Golf & Country Club 46
Magna Marbella Golf 47

BUDGET TIPS 49

🌐 Accommodation 49
La Villa Marbella 49
La Morada Mas Hermosa Hotel 50
Hotel-Apartamentos Puerta de Aduares 51
Vincci Seleccion Estrella del Mar 52
Princesa Playa Hotel Apartamentos 53

🌐 Eating & Drinking 54
Tempora 54
Rendez Vous 55
Stuzzikini 56
La Taberna del Pintxo 57
Bar El Estrecho 57

🌐 Shopping 58
Puerto Banus Street Market 59
El Corte Ingles 59
Marina Banus 60
Centro Comercial La Cañada 61
Zoco del Sol Market 62

KNOW BEFORE YOU GO 63

🌐 Entry Requirements 63
🌐 Health Insurance 63
🌐 Travelling with Pets 64
🌐 Airports 65

- Airlines 66
- Currency 67
- Banking & ATMs 67
- Credit Cards 67
- Tourist Taxes 68
- Reclaiming VAT 68
- Tipping policy 69
- Mobile Phones 69
- Dialling Code 70
- Emergency Numbers 71
- Public Holidays 71
- Time Zone 72
- Daylight Savings Time 72
- School Holidays 73
- Trading Hours 73
- Driving Laws 73
- Drinking Laws 74
- Smoking Laws 74
- Electricity 75
- Food & Drink 75

MARBELLA TRAVEL GUIDE

Marbella

Marbella on the Costa del Sol in Spain is the destination of choice for the rich and famous. In Marbella and its neighbour Puerto Banús you will rub shoulders with international celebrities at the super-smart beach clubs and can dance until dawn at the areas famous nightspots.

MARBELLA TRAVEL GUIDE

Marbella and Puerto Banús are linked by the five kilometre Avenida Bulevar Príncipe Alfonso de Hohenlohe, locally known as the Golden Mile. There are several five star luxury hotels with their luxurious tropical gardens that reach down to the sea and their private beach clubs. Halfway along the Golden Mile (set back a few hundred metres) is the Royal Palace of King Fahd. The late king of Saudi Arabia used to come to his palace every year until his death in 2005 bringing a very welcome injection of millions of euros into the local area.

Marbella itself has two distinct parts; the newer area stretches down to the port and marina which in turn leads into the wide promenade. There are many bars and shops in this area along the seafront which faces the flat, sandy beach. On the beach there are plenty of sunbeds and thatched sun umbrellas to hire for a day's relaxation in the

MARBELLA TRAVEL GUIDE

sun. The Old Town sits further back up a slight hill and is typically Spanish with plazas, one way streets and dead ends. It is much easier to walk round the Old Town than to drive.

A Spanish ambience remains in Marbella despite the many hotels, restaurants and shops that cater to foreign visitors. It is still possible to find a coffee or beer and a snack for a couple of euros if you look in the right places, but if you want to pay a week's salary for an evenings entertainment you can find that as well.

The main street of Marbella sees expensive sports cars pass through all day long, but in the middle of all this pristine bodywork and glass are wizened Spanish men winding their way through the traffic on old, dusty mopeds. Designer boutiques with guards on the door sit

MARBELLA TRAVEL GUIDE

side by side with euro bazaars and mini-markets where señoras dressed in black (as well as tourists) poke though the goods looking for the best buys.

The town itself and the outskirts of Marbella have become home to many clinics where it is not just the stars that come for plastic surgery treatments to enhance their looks. Many health tourists come for facelifts, nose and boob jobs and other processes that try to turn back the clock. And there's no better place to recuperate than in the warm Spanish sun.

Marbella has an established cultural schedule, mainly in the summer but for most of the year there is an event happening somewhere round the town. In addition to concerts there are exhibitions, recitals and readings. There is always a big music choice from opera to jazz and

MARBELLA TRAVEL GUIDE

reggae to classical, all manner of tribute bands play to packed audiences as well as some of today's stars performing in person. Some events are in small exclusive venues and others are in places like the local bullring that holds thousands of people. One thing they have in common though especially in the summer is the promise of listening to good music and dancing under a blanket of stars in the warmth of a Mediterranean evening.

Marbella Fair (Feria de San Bernabe) is held in June every year when the streets of the Old Town are lined with stalls while just outside the town a huge fairground with death-defying rides and ear-shattering music goes on until the early hours of the morning. It is a great opportunity to dress up and mingle with the crowds as families, friends and sweethearts come together to take part in one of the party highlights of the year. Several events take place in the days leading up to the fair with processions of horses, floats and people parading through the town. There are fireworks and dancing, marching bands and lots of eating and drinking which all blend together to make a visit to the fair in Spain one to remember.

🌎 Planning Your Stay

The Costa del Sol is located in southern Spain in the province of Málaga in the self-governing community of Andalucia. The Costa del Sol spans 160 kilometres from Nerja to Manilva with Marbella in the western-third. Marbella is situated on the Mediterranean Sea and sits under the watchful eye of La Concha, which stands at 1,215 metres high and is part of the Sierra Blanca range of mountains.

MARBELLA TRAVEL GUIDE

The municipality of Marbella extends along the coast for 44 kilometres and has a population of 140,000 permanent inhabitants. It is a transient town though with people of all nationalities passing through every week. Some stay a while and find temporary work, earn a few euros and then move on; others make Spain their home and stay forever.

The lifeblood of many businesses depends on the international tourists that visit Marbella to visit the playgrounds of the wealthy and to enjoy the wonderful climate. Through the peak summer months of July, August and September around one million overnight stays are recorded in Marbella every year.

The closest airport to Marbella is Málaga International Airport approximately 60 kilometres away to the east. Budget flights from all over Europe arrive in Málaga

MARBELLA TRAVEL GUIDE

bringing in millions of visitors every year. A multi-million euro expansion plan and second runway in recent years means that Málaga Airport is ready to receive even more travellers in the future.

To get to Marbella from Malaga airport means hiring a car (typically super cheap from about €15/day) or taking a bus or taxi. There isn't a train station in Marbella, the nearest one is in Fuengirola 20 kilometres away and that is only a local line, although it does stop at the airport. There is a direct coach link between Málaga and Marbella which uses the toll road and it is quick and easy. Other bus routes go along the coast road with many stops and are usually quite crowded in the peak months.

Road links are good with the new Málaga bypass meaning anyone driving down from the north of Spain doesn't have to battle through Málaga city centre traffic to get to Marbella. The old coast road runs the length of the Costa Del Sol and although it is a dual carriageway it can get very crowded and is better avoided unless absolutely necessary.

🌍 Climate & Weather

Marbella has a Mediterranean climate that is usually mild with dry, hot summers and moderate winters although the peaks of the Sierra Blanca do get a dusting of snow from time to time. The same peaks protect Marbella from icy cold weather blowing in through the winter months and this gives the town a very pleasant micro-climate.

Spring and autumn are the nicest seasons to visit if a hectic sightseeing schedule is on your agenda. The weather is pleasant but not too hot and of course

MARBELLA TRAVEL GUIDE

everywhere is slightly less crowded than in the peak summer months. The temperature can reach highs of 24°C in both seasons and dip down to a low of 11°C at night. It can rain in spring and autumn but more often than not it will be a short, heavy downpour.

Summer is hot, hot, hot! The forecast will give a high of 30°C but in reality in direct sun the mercury can reach 40°C and above. The sand can be blisteringly hot so always remember to wear sandals to the beach and wherever you go take lots of high factor sun cream and plenty of water to drink. The locals are easy to spot in the summer, while visitors cook their sun-starved skin to a nice shade of lobster-red the residents walk on the shady side of the street and always sit under umbrellas at the bars. They always looked relaxed in the heat and have no nasty strap marks or giveaway peeling shoulders!

MARBELLA TRAVEL GUIDE

In Spain summer officially starts on the night of San Juan, the 23rd June - 24th June. On beaches everywhere bonfires are lit and families and friends gather together to eat, drink and make merry all night to welcome in another scorching summer. At midnight tradition says you should jump over the bonfire three times to burn away your problems and then run into the sea to cleanse the spirit.

As autumn moves into winter the Spanish people bring out their fur coats, thick jumpers and scarves which makes you think it is really cold. Even in December the high can be around 16º C although nights can be quite nippy and temperatures drop to around 7ºC. The winter sun is still pleasant and in a sheltered spot in the middle of the day it can still be warm enough not to need a jumper.

MARBELLA TRAVEL GUIDE

The micro-climate in the area means that Marbella has 320 days of sunshine per year, with 11 hours a day in the summer and about half that figure in winter.

MARBELLA TRAVEL GUIDE

Sightseeing

🌐 Selwo Adventure Safari Park

A7 highway km 162, 5

Estepona

29680 Málaga

Tel: +34 952 57 77 73

www.selwo.es/

MARBELLA TRAVEL GUIDE

Selwo Adventure Safari Park is a great day out for all the family. The park is well designed and you get a real feel of being out in the wild.

To enter and leave the different territories you pass through enormous wooden gates into the Canyon of the Birds. This is a vast area enclosed by almost invisible netting where the birds fly free among tropical plants and trees and the water sprays give the sense of a steamy jungle.

Cross over the Bridge of Africa and you can get a bird's eye view of the park. The rope and wood bridge sways gently as you cross over high above the lake, 100 metres below. Spread out below are over 2,000 animals from all five continents and there are opportunities to see many of them close at hand by taking the safari tour in the zebra-striped all-terrain trucks. From vantage points on the way round you can see the animals living as they would in the wild. There are no cages and no obvious fencing which gives a real safari feel to the tour.

If you get hungry there is the Fast Food Korongo Restaurant and the Lake Kiosk where energy reserves can be replenished. For a really special night under the stars there are 23 well-appointed cabins at the Selwo Lodge Hotel where you fall sleep listening to the sounds of the wild animals.

The park is open from 10am until about 6pm and later in the summer holidays. In the winter months the park is closed on some days so check before you go. There is an excellent day-to-day calendar on the website. Admission proices are €24.50 adult and €17 for children and OAP's.

MARBELLA TRAVEL GUIDE

There are online discounts and various family packages available.

🌐 Museum of Contemporary Spanish Engraving

Calle Hospital de Bazán

Marbella

29601 Málaga

Tel: +34 952 76 57 41

www.mgec.es/

The Museum of Contemporary Spanish Engraving opened in 1992 after a donation of 1,350 works by two Spanish authors. Marbella Town Hall gave permission to use the old Hospital Bazán with its Renaissance architecture to house the collection and there are now around 4,000 works in the museum. Prestigious names such as Picasso, Conongar, Miró, Barceló, Tàpies and Caruso are just a few that can be found representing this type of Spanish art. There also many temporary exhibitions and music and art related activities.

The museum is open on Mondays 10am to 2pm, Tuesdays to Fridays 10am to 2.30pm and 5pm to 8.30pm and Saturdays 10am to 2pm. In summer the museum stays open until 10pm Tuesdays to Fridays.

Puerto Banús & Marina

Nueva Andalucía

29660 Málaga

A few kilometres southwest of Marbella is the town of Puerto Banús with its swishy apartments and houses, chic hotels and a 915-berth marina.

MARBELLA TRAVEL GUIDE

The marina was the brainchild of José Banús, a local developer, and designed by Noldi Schreck who was in part responsible for the design of Beverly Hills. The marina complex opened in May 1970 and 1700 guests got through 22 kilos of beluga caviar.

The guest list for the opening was star-studded with Prince Rainier and Princess Grace of Monaco, Hugh Hefner, the Aga Khan and Dr Christiaan Barnard being just a few of the attendees. They were entertained by a very young Julio Iglesias who got the princely sum of 125 thousand pesetas for his performance. Iglesias probably never dreamed that years later he would be one of Spain's biggest stars and have a luxurious home in the hills overlooking that same marina.

MARBELLA TRAVEL GUIDE

The town is the place to see and be seen, international celebrities and the world's jet set flock here in the summer months and the waterfront parking spaces are full of Lamborghini's, Porches and Ferrari's. The multi-million pound yachts and cruisers bob gently up and down with their smartly uniformed staff polishing and cleaning every surface waiting for their wealthy owners to return.

The marina is surrounded by apartments built in typical Mediterranean style and is laid out like a small village with cobbled streets full of designer shops and expensive restaurants. Armed guards stand at the doors of the most exclusive jewellers and car showrooms keeping a watchful eye on anyone that enters.

Across the main coast road from Puerto Banús is Nueva Andalucía and on a Saturday morning this is where the

MARBELLA TRAVEL GUIDE

market is held in and around Centro Plaza and the bullring. Old and new, bargains and the not so cheap can all be found here. Clothes, shoes, furniture, bric-a-brac and a good selection of junk are the order of the day along with fruits, vegetables and plants. Trading usually starts about 9am through to 2pm.

Another one of Spain's well known son's is Salvador Dali and it is Dali that created the three ton rhinoceros statue that stands on one on the town's roundabouts. Dali made the sculpture in 1956 for one of his films and in 2004 it was given pride of place in Puerto Banús.

🌍 Júzcar Smurf Village

Serrania de Ronda, 29642 Málaga

Tel: +34 952 18 35 67

www.júzcar.es/

MARBELLA TRAVEL GUIDE

Picturesque Spanish mountain villages in the Ronda area usually have white-washed houses nestling against a backdrop of forest.

Not this one as Sony Pictures came to visit in 2011 and painted the whole town blue for the premiere of the Smurfs 3D film. Using 4,000 litres of paint everything in the village was painted Smurf colour, right down to the church and the gravestones. Sony did offer to repaint the village white but the inhabitants voted to keep the colour and visitor figures leapt from just 300 annually to 80,000 in the six months following the film's release.

Even without the pretty shade of blue Júzcar would be an attractive village. Situated inland about 40 kilometres from Marbella the drive takes you up the winding mountain road and into the Serrania de Ronda. The scenery is spectacular with mountains all around and small waterfalls cascading down by the edge of the road.

Júzcar village is quaint with steep streets and oddly shaped chimneys sticking up from ancient rooftops and the most unique building in the village is the 16th century Church of Saint Catherine. There is an ancient Tin Factory to visit and many beautifully crafted items to buy made from hemp and locally grown cork. Stay a while and have lunch in one of the little restaurants; the rabbit cooked with loads of garlic is a speciality of the area.

🌍 Marbella Old Town & Orange Tree Square

The pedestrianised cobbled streets of Marbella's Old Town are in complete contrast to the four lane main artery

MARBELLA TRAVEL GUIDE

of Avenida Ricardo Soriano just a few hundred metres away. The Old Town of Marbella includes the ancient city walls and the layout of the city is almost the same as in the 16th century. There are intriguing little shops selling a mixture of everyday necessities, locally made goods and luxury items.

Every corner reveals another intriguing passageway or square to admire, some of which are very tiny. Orange Tree Square is the place to head to and this is where the Tourist Office is situated with some very nice bars and restaurants just waiting to be visited. The square has historical buildings on three sides comprising the town hall, the Mayor's house and the Chapel of Santiago.

To the side of the Old Town make a point of finding Calle Rio and Calle San Cristobal. The streets are so narrow that you can stand in the middle and touch the houses on both sides with outstretched arms. The residents here have an amazing display of plants and flowers that fill the street and balconies with every shade of green and a profusion of brightly coloured blooms.

🌐 Church of Our Lady

Plaza de la Iglesia

Marbella

29601Málaga

Tel: +34 952 77 31 36

www.diocesismalaga.es/

Close to Orange Tree Square in the Old Town in Marbella is the Church of Our Lady of the Incarnation. This is a popular visitor spot in the Old Town and dates back to 1485 when the Catholic Kings re-conquered Marbella.

The church was constructed in 1505 and one its most striking features is the bell tower, reaching up to a height to around 33 metres. The tower has four sections with clocks and bells and the oldest bell is on the east, all this is topped by a pyramid shaped tiled spire. The church is open from 8pm to 10pm for observation and prayer.

Ronda & Tajo Gorge

Ronda 29400

Tel: +34 952 18 71 19

www.turismoderonda.es/

The town of Ronda is about 60 kilometres inland from Marbella and Puerto Banús.

The road up is excellent although winding and there are several restaurants on the way plus various stopping

MARBELLA TRAVEL GUIDE

points to take some super photos. Ronda is at an altitude of between 600-700 metres high in the Serrania de Ronda and in winter can get completely cut off by snow. As you climb higher there are snow warning signs at the side of the road, which always seems bizarre in the summer heat.

Ronda is a pretty town with a lot of history behind it. Park on the edge of the town and walk through the narrow streets towards the famous Tajo Gorge and the Bull Ring. It is one of the oldest cities in Spain and archaeological findings put the first signs of civilisation somewhere in the Neolithic age. There is so much to do and see in Ronda it is almost impossible to list. The Tourist Office is opposite the Bull Ring and is the best place to start. Guided tours of the city are on offer or if you prefer to go at your own pace, there is a discounted Visitors Pass. This gives entry into some of the most popular attractions including the Visitor Centre at the Tajo Gorge, two museums and the Arab Baths.

The Bull Ring in Ronda is one of the biggest and most monumental in Spain. The building of the Bull Ring took six years and the fighting arena has a diameter of 66 metres. The two tiers of seating are under 68 archways held up by 136 Tuscany columns and despite the purpose of the structure there is a definite beauty and grace to it. Inside there is a small museum dedicated to bull fighting and a collection of old military weapons.

Tajo Gorge

The view from the Puento Nuevo (New Bridge) over the Gorge is stunning and you can walk all the way round the edge admiring the rolling countryside stretching away towards the mountains from different angles. The bridge took 42 years to build and from the start of construction in 1751 there were 50 builders who died during the process. The bridge is 120 metres high and has been used for various purposes including a prison over the years and the central arch conceals a chamber that was used as torture chamber during the Civil War. It is said that soldiers on both sides of the war threw captured opponents from the chamber to their death on the rocks below. There is an exhibition that is open to the public in the chamber telling the story of the history and construction of the bridge.

🌐 Grazalema & Ubrique Villages

Marbella and Puerto Banús are the most well known destinations on this part of the Costa del Sol, but spare a thought for some of the wonderful inland destinations.

MARBELLA TRAVEL GUIDE

There are lots of pretty villages nestled in the mountains that shelter the coast and it really is worth spending a day or two exploring. To get to Grazalema head inland towards Ronda but miss out the town and take the Algodonales road and then turn off towards Grazalema.

Depending on the time of year there could be vast fields of sunflowers, their smiley yellow faces following the sun all day long. The drive takes you through some of the cork forests and this part of Andalucia is one of the world's biggest producers of cork. It takes nine years for the bark to grow thick enough to be harvested and you can see many different stages of cork growth in the trees as you drive past. Somewhere in the vast forest cork is always being cut as there enough trees for it to be an on-going business on a nine year cycle.

Grazalema

This is only a small village with around 2000 inhabitants but it is incredibly popular with tourists and artists. Many painters come and stay here to take advantage of the clear, natural light and wonderful views. Park in the car park at the far end of the village and admire the view from the lookout point. From this vantage point the view stretches for mile after mile back down towards the coast. A walk down into the village will take you past tiny village houses, their front patios full of brightly coloured geraniums and glossy green plants. There is a small tourist office and several shops selling a variety of daily items and souvenirs.

In the central square there are restaurants whose tables and chairs are all side by side under shady umbrellas and canopies, just right for enjoying an ice-cold beer underneath. Try some of the specialties like oxtail stew, black pudding made with rice or deep fried aubergine crisps drizzled with honey.

To get to Ubrique leave Grazelema behind you but don't go back towards Ronda. Take the road to Villaluenga del Rosario, onwards to Benoacaz and down the hairpin bends into Ubrique. The village of Villaluenga is tiny but there are several factory shops selling goat and sheep cheese and other related products.

Ubrique

The town of Ubrique is perched on a steep hillside and is famous for its amount of leather factories and shops. The population is around 17,000 and many of these people work in leather related industries of which there are over three hundred. It was the Romans who founded Ubrique and started the history of leather making in this pretty Spanish village. The village of Ubrique is now known world-wide as a location for top quality leather goods and many designers seek out the small factories to make their very expensive bags and other goods.

There is a small Leather Museum on Avenida de Herrera Oria where leather working machinery can be seen and a guided tour be taken. The walls are hung with works of art, not painted but make of tooled leather. There are some superb examples of leather goods to see as well as displays of how leather is made into bags. Admission is free but a small donation to the upkeep of the museum is always welcome.

The small church of San Antonio is worth visiting with its pretty belfry and Baroque style. Behind the church is a lookout point which gives an excellent panoramic view of the town and countryside below. Wander back down through the maze of streets and you will be spoilt for choice at the amount of shops to choose from and the beautiful goods on display. The main street is the pretty tree-lined Avenida de España, some of which is traffic free. There are dozens of bars and restaurants scattered along here and all throughout the town where a wide choice of Spanish food to suit all tastes and budgets is available.

 Constitution Park

Avenida de la Fontanilla

Marbella

29601 Málaga

MARBELLA TRAVEL GUIDE

Join the locals and take a walk through this Moroccan style park. Constitution Park is only a few minutes away from the Marbella promenade but offers a welcome respite from the searing sun that beats relentlessly down on the sea front. It is an oasis of calm and tranquility which makes it hard to believe that not far away the chaos of Spanish life goes on as usual. It is a great place to for children and there is a well-designed playground as well as an ice-cream parlour. There is a small open air auditorium and through the summer months there are many concerts and exhibitions held in the park

In the summer from about 8pm onwards the park will fill up with extended families bringing their children out to let off steam as the day cools down. With a three month school holiday there is no such thing as bedtime and even the babies and toddlers will still be out until the early hours. The park is beautifully kept and the fir trees soar above the beds of seasonal plants that bring colour to the park all the year round.

Bonsai Museum

Avenida del Doctor Maiz Vinals

Parque Arroyo de la Represa

29600 Marbella

Málaga

Tel: +34 952 86 29 26

The Bonsai Museum in Marbella was created by Miguel Angel Garcia and he still lovingly tends to his miniature trees on a daily basis including the Acebuche Olive which is a mere 300 years young. The collection is known as one of the finest of its kind in the world and some of the

MARBELLA TRAVEL GUIDE

other specimens are over 500 years old. The museum is set partly over a lake and turtles can be seen basking lazily in the water below waiting for any bread that might come their way. There is a feeling of calm inside the museum with the sound of the water trickling over the rocks that were specially brought in from nearby El Torcal Country Park in Antequera. For a peaceful retreat from the strong Spanish sun it is worth a stroll up the slight hill to admire these dwarf plants and trees.

Opening hours are 10.30 to 1.30 all year round and 4pm to 7pm. From the middle of July to the end of August it is 5pm to 8.30pm. Admission fee is €4 per adult and €2 for children.

MARBELLA TRAVEL GUIDE

🌑 Horse & Carriage Tour

Alameda Park

29601 Marbella

Málaga

A lovely way to see the main attractions in the town of Marbella is to take a gentle ride in a horse and carriage and right next to the Alameda Park there is an equine taxi rank. These beautifully kept animals will take you around the town accompanied by the jingle of harness and the clip clop of hooves which is a lovely relaxed way to travel. Tours last for one hour or 30 minutes and cost around €40 or €20 respectively. The routes can vary but the tour takes in the beaches, the historic Old Town and the centre of the new town, Marbella Castle and Los Lagos amongst other sites.

 Estepona

Estepona is virtually surrounded by the Sierra Bermeja massif which is near nearly 1500 metres at its highest point. The rocks have a reddish tinge and this comes from periodite, an igneous rock. This area is the largest mass of periodite found in southern Europe as well as being home to the only forest of Spanish firs found on this type of rock.

This backdrop to Estepona town is stunning, with thick forests of deep green fir trees carpeting the Sierra Bermeja, hiding white villages and picturesque places to stop and admire the view from. From the highest points there are magnificent views across to North Africa and the Atlas and Rif mountains. Lower down towards the sea there are orchards of citrus fruit, meadows for grazing and then areas of scrubland where the land meets the sea.

MARBELLA TRAVEL GUIDE

The Playa de Rada, which won a prestigious EC blueflag in 2009 stretches for around 2.5 kilometres from the giant Carrefour superstore at the eastern end to the pretty little marina at the other. The beach itself is wide, flat and sandy with a beautiful promenade all the way along that is just right for a gentle stroll. The main coastal road divides the beach from the town but thanks to the new toll road the amount of traffic is far less than it used to be. Once across the road the first three streets of the town are parallel to the beach and some are traffic-free. There are many bars and restaurants in this area serving a mixture of traditional and international food and drink. Behind these streets is a maze of smaller, narrow streets hiding a wealth of small shops and boutiques.

MARBELLA TRAVEL GUIDE

The town centre is quite small but there are many urbanisations stretching out to each side and up the slopes behind the town. There is everything here for a super Spanish holiday without quite as much frenetic hustle and bustle of the more popular resorts closer to Málaga.

At the western end of the town is Estepona Marina where there are lots of tapas bars and restaurants', parking is easy as there is a car park at the end of the marina. Estepona town is not really known for its night life but there are several bars and clubs in the marina that stay open until the small hours and play very loud music. The marina is pretty and in the evening when the suns sinks over the horizon and the lights come on it is a pleasant place for a leisurely meal.

For history lovers the church of Los Remedios in Plaza San Francisco in Estepona is worth visiting, built in the 18th century the church has been used as a monastery and as a hospice over the years. Local sandstone was used to build the church which is rich in iron ore and the pieces of iron are easily visible in the walls as you walk around the exterior. The entrance doorway is impressive with a particularly attractive statue of the Virgin Mary surrounded by the sun, moon and stars.

Museums of Palaeontology, Ethnography, Bullfighting, Image & Sound

C/ Matías Prats, Plaza de Toros, Estepona

29680 Málaga

Tel: +34 952 80 71 48

MARBELLA TRAVEL GUIDE

Estepona Bull Ring is within walking distance of the town and promenade. There are four small museums here that give an insight into various aspects of Spanish history.

Admission is free and the opening hours are 10am to 2pm all year round, 4pm to 6pm in winter and 5pm to 6.30pm in summer.

The four museums are:

Museum of Ethnography: A collection of some 2,000 pieces sharing Estepona's past customs and lifestyle.

Antonio Ordóñez Museum of Bullfighting: Learn all one of Spain's most traditional sports with this fascinating collection of bullfighting memorabilia and some stunning matadors costumes.

MARBELLA TRAVEL GUIDE

Museum of Image and Sound: The Edgar Neville Hall has an amazing collection of projectors and cameras and in the María Isbert Hall and Spring Music Hall there are mementoes from visiting artists and their concerts.

Museum of Palaeontology: Scholars from all over Europe use the marine and mollusc collections here. There are also ten specimens of dinosaurs from Argentina and an example of a unique coral reef.

Parque San Isidro & Necropolis Visitor Centre

Los Pedregales, Estepona, 29680 Málaga

Five kilometres outside of the town set in a large country park is the reconstruction of an archaeological site.

MARBELLA TRAVEL GUIDE

Thanks to the construction of the new toll road at the beginning of the 21st century experts discovered several bodies and five tombs in the Estepona area. All these exciting finds were moved to Los Pedregales so everyone could see first-hand the stone beads, tools, arrow heads, axes and pottery that had been uncovered. A new visitor centre was created in the park which is also used for small concerts which are held regularly. The park has some lovely areas for walking and studying the flora and fauna as well as areas for picnics and barbeques.

🌐 Funny Beach Amusement Park

A7 Km 184

Marbella

29603 Málaga

Tel: +34 952 823 359

MARBELLA TRAVEL GUIDE

www.funnybeach.com

Funny Beach Amusement Park is easy to find as there is a giant inflatable Coca Cola can that sits at the entrance. There is loads of fun for all the family here, the parking is easy and it is right by the edge of the wide sandy beach. There is go-karting for adults and children as well as two-seater karts, parasailing, jet skis, banana boat rides, water skiing, trampolines and a whole host of other activities.

Food and drink is never a problem as there are three great places to choose from depending on what you fancy. For a relaxed lunch the beach bar has plenty of tables to choose from and a wide and varied menu with lots of freshly caught fish and shellfish.

The restaurant is slightly more upmarket and offers the same excellent service and quality. The beach club has luxurious sunbeds with canopies and is the place to go to be spoilt. There is a full programme of events and music on through the summer months so check on the website before you go.

Funny Beach is open 365 days a year from 11am right through until 11pm and the beach club stays open to 2am. Charges vary per activity but all the prices are clearly listed on the Funny Beach website.

🌐 Boat Trips from Marbella to Puerto Banus

www.fly-blue.com/

Get on board a water taxi and enjoy the breezy sea air on

MARBELLA TRAVEL GUIDE

the trip between Marbella and Puerto Banús. The boats leave from the marinas of the respective towns every hour and the trip lasts for an hour. There are beautiful views along the coastline as you sail gently between the two towns passing the five star hotels on the Golden Mile and luxury mansions sprawling at the foot of La Concha. The ferry runs from 1st March until 30th November and adult single ticket is €8.50, child €5. There are slight discounts for return tickets.

For a longer sailing trip Fly Blue have a catamaran that takes you out into the Mediterranean Sea and offers chances to swim in the clear blue water and maybe see dolphins. There is a free bar for an hour while on board and opportunities to try out some water sports. The trips depart twice daily from each port and the cost is €50 for adults and €25 for children. The trip lasts for three hours.

# Alcornocales Natural Park & Cortes de la Frontera

Serrania de Ronda

29380 Málaga

Tel: +34 952 15 40 00

www.cortesdelafrontera.es/

Cortes de la Frontera is a village that lays hidden deep in the forest in the Alcornocales Natural Park. The village is small but has its own train station approximately two kilometres away from the centre. Unfortunately there are not any trains from Marbella but a drive through the great expanses of uninhabited Mediterranean forests more than makes up for it. The train actually runs from La Linea near Gibraltar up to Ronda and there are several stopping points on the way. It is an excellent way of seeing the beauty that this part of Andalucía has to offer.

MARBELLA TRAVEL GUIDE

Cortes might only be small but like every Spanish village it has its share of festivals. In June the parade for the Virgin of the Rosary winds through the streets and there is also a fair dedicated to horses.

In August the village celebrates the fair of San Roque and San Sebastián, the towns patron saints. There are dances, contests and a cattle fair plus the release of a bull into the streets. Naturally being Spain there is a plethora of colour and sound, accompanied by lots of food and drink.

There are many places to try the local delicacies in the village and veal is a popular choice, along with locally produced hams, honey and cheese. In autumn wild boar is always on the menu for anyone wanting to try something different.

The park of Los Alcornocales spreads across the provinces of Málaga and Cadiz and covers 17 municipalities. Alcornocales means cork oak groves and it isn't hard to work out why. Cork is big business and Spain is the biggest producer of cork in the world, much of it coming from Andalucía. The men that harvest the cork spend two years training to learn their craft and the bark is cut on a nine year cycle.

🌍 Golf Courses

Andalucía is famous for its golf courses and there are almost 100 of them, with two thirds being on the Costa del Sol, or Costa del Golf as it is sometimes called. Golfing is big business and for visitors wishing to play a few rounds

MARBELLA TRAVEL GUIDE

or get some practice in the choice is huge. Four of the courses on the Costa del Sol are in Europe's top ten including Los Naranjos in Marbella. The majority of the courses have 18 holes but there are some nine-hole courses. Green fees and buggy hire are quite reasonable and there are many companies that organise golfing packages.

Los Naranjos

Plaza Cibeles

Nueva Andalucía

29660, Marbella

Tel: +34 952 81 52 06

www.losnaranjos.com/

Los Naranjos opened in 1977 and was designed by Robert Trent Jones Sr. Many improvements have been made over the years and the course offers amateurs and professionals the chance to play a few rounds only a short putt from Puerto Banús.

Marbella Golf & Country Club

Ctra de Cádiz, N-340 Km.188

29604 Marbella

Tel: + 34 952 83 05 00

www.marbellagolf.com

Marbella Golf offers one of the most challenging courses on the coast, and is only a five minute drive from the centre of Marbella. There is a putting green, three tennis courts and a shop as well as the club house and restaurant with beautiful views across the immaculately manicured grass.

Magna Marbella Golf

Calle Calderón de la Barca

29660 Marbella

Tel. +34 952 92 92 49

www.magnamarbellagolf.com/

This is one of the regions nine-hole golf courses and was designed by José Maria Elguezabal. It is quite a demanding course with many water hazards but can be got round in less than two hours with with some very precise playing. For refreshments and a bird's eye view across the green the Millionaires Club and Restaurant will cater to your every need.

MARBELLA TRAVEL GUIDE

Budget Tips

 Accommodation

La Villa Marbella

Calle Principe 10, Old Historic Town, 29600 Marbella

(+34) 952 76 62 20

http://www.lavillamarbella.com/

Averaging 150€ per night, depending upon the season, La

MARBELLA TRAVEL GUIDE

Villa Marbella is a great place to stay while visiting Marbella.

Its location is ideal with Orange Square only a three-minute walk away and Puerto Banus only a ten-minute walk. This is a romantic hotel that offers free breakfast to its guests, as well as complementary WiFi and laundry facilities. Guests can also enjoy the bar and lounge as well as the scenic rooftop terrace. There is a babysitter service as well as airport transfers.

La Morada Mas Hermosa Hotel

Calle Montenebros 16

Casco Antiguo, 29601 Marbella

+34 952 92 44 67

http://www.lamoradamashermosa.com/

MARBELLA TRAVEL GUIDE

La Morada Mas Hermosa is a beautiful hotel located in the Old Town of Marbella.

It is situated on a pedestrian only street, and you can park in the nearby Mercado Municipal, only a 200-meter walk from the hotel. Guests can get a breakfast basket delivered to their rooms, or take their breakfast in the common area. Rooms average 100€ per night depending on the type of room and time of year. The hotel also offers airport transfers.

Hotel-Apartamentos Puerta de Aduares

C/ Aduar, 18, 29601

Marbella

(+34) 952 82 13 12

http://www.puertadeaduares.com/

MARBELLA TRAVEL GUIDE

This centrally located hotel offers roomy apartment-like accommodations on a budget. Averaging 100€, the "rooms" are a steal with their kitchenettes and terraces or balconies. Parking is free. The beaches are only a five-minute walk from the hotel; which sits on a quiet, residential street. The owners are friendly as well.

Vincci Seleccion Estrella del Mar

Carretera Nacional 340 Km 191, Las Chapas, 29604

Marbella

(+34) 951 05 39 70

http://www.vinccihoteles.com

This is a resort with every amenity you can imagine averaging 150€ per night. The resort is located just besides the sea and has beach access as well as an outdoor swimming pool. It is 5 miles (8 km) from the center of Marbella in the area of Elviria Las Chapas. Its 137 rooms and suites reflect a modern Mediterranean style with a bit of Arab influence. This is the hotel to book if you are on a slight budget but want to feel like high society.

Princesa Playa Hotel Apartamentos

Paseo Maritimo, s/n, 29600 Marbella

(+34) 952 82 09 44

http://www.hotelprincesaplaya.com/en/index.htm

The Princesa Playa Hotel Apartamentos is a value, averaging 75€ per night and located right on the beach with only a five-minute walk to the Old Town. It offers 64 rooms and 36 apartments as well as a restaurant, a terrace bar and outdoors swimming pool. It was completely refurbished in 2006, but is still an older hotel; so if you are looking for something very modern, you might want to consider looking elsewhere. Still, it is a great value and spotlessly clean.

 Eating & Drinking

Tempora

Tetuan 9a

29601 Marbella

(+34) 95 285 7933

Tempora is a newer restaurant in the Old Town of Marbella with a name that means, "season" in Spanish.

MARBELLA TRAVEL GUIDE

Despite its youth, this quaint establishment has already garnered the respect and adoration of both locals and tourists alike. The owner's philosophy is to cook with fresh, seasonal ingredients in order to prepare and serve dishes of the highest possible quality.

Every day, Chef Abraham Garrote Costa accompanies owner, Andrés Perdiguero to the local market in search for the ingredients that will suit their menu for the day. Since they use only the produce that is "in season," you will most likely find a different menu with each visit. To find the restaurant, find the horse fountain across from Parque de Alameda. Once at the fountain, Tetuan is the first street on your right. Tempora is on the left side of the street, in the middle of the block.

Expect to pay an average of 20€ per entrée. Reservations are accepted.

Rendez Vous

Avenida del Prado Nueva Andalucia

29660 Marbella

(+34) 952 813 912

http://rendezvous-marbella.com/

Rendez Vous is a French bistro located in the heart of Marbella. The owners, Mikael and Céline, are known for their traditional French dishes and their macarons. Do not be intimidated by its fancy interior.

It is budget friendly while classy. Rendez Vous is open on Tuesdays through Sundays from 9 a.m. until 5 p.m. for breakfast and lunch. On Sundays, they offer a brunch service. Every Friday, from 7 p.m. until 9 p.m., the restaurant offers champagne tasting paired with some of Chef Mikael's dishes.

Stuzzikini

c/ Alderete 5,

29600 Marbella

(+34) 952 775 994

http://www.stuzzikini.com/

Stuzzikini is the project of Chef Robert, who has spent his formative cooking years in Italy, Spain, and England. He serves Italian food that makes people think they are in Sardinia. The dishes are unique but still carry a trace of their homelands. Atmosphere at Stuzzikini is relaxed but adheres to a high attention to detail that includes charming Italian music. Stuzzikini is open daily except for

Tuesdays, from 7:00 p.m. until close. Reservations are recommended.

La Taberna del Pintxo

Avenida Miguel Cano 7, 29600 Marbella

(+34) 952 829 321

http://www.latabernadelpintxo.com/

The Basque regions equivalent of "tapas" is a "pinxto," which is this Basque restaurants specialty. La Taberna del Pintxo offer two categories of pinxtos - cold and hot.

The cold pinxtos can be purchased at the bar while the hot pinxtos are served at the table. The cuisine includes flavors from both the north and south of Spain as well as ingredients of the best quality. They are also known for serving good Spanish wine.

Bar El Estrecho

Calle San Lazaro 12

Old Town, 29601 Marbella

(+34) 95 277 0004

http://www.barelestrecho.es/

Open since 1954, this tapas restaurant serves traditional Spanish cuisine in a charming atmosphere. It is slightly hidden, in a narrow alley in old town, but this should not discourage you from looking for it. Service is consistently friendly and accommodating. Prices range from $5 to $15.

Shopping

Considering the fact that Marbella is one of those destinations where people go to see and be seen, one of the most popular things to shop for is clothing. Although it has its share of high-end shops, Marbella also offers its visitors fashionable European style apparel at more reasonable prices than in many other European cities.

If you are looking for something in particular, Marbella's megastores like El Corte Ingles will not disappoint. But the best way to find hidden treasures at bargain prices is simply to stroll through town and stop at one of the many local merchants or street markets.

Puerto Banus Street Market

Boulevard de La Fama

(Parking is at Centro Plaza mall on Calle Camilo Jose Cela)

Just a short walk from the centre of Puerto Banus and located near the bullring is the Saturday Puerto Banus street market. This is a great place to buy souvenirs and just about anything else you can imagine. Start at the bullring and head down to the port as you browse the spices, clothes, vegetables, and furniture. Parking can be congested, so be sure to arrive early or late. Although it opens at 9 a.m., many stalls aren't ready until 10 a.m. It closes at 2 p.m.

El Corte Ingles

Calle Ramón Areces

Puerto Banus

(+34) 952 909 990

http://www.elcorteingles.es/

El Corte Inglés is the major department store in Marbella and is the largest shopping chain in Spain and all of Europe. It is here that you can find everything you need, including brands from the best names in fashion. There is also a supermarket (Hipercor), optician, and travel agency.

El Corte Ingles is open Monday through Saturday from 10:00 a.m. to 10:00 p.m. in the winter and daily from 10:30 a.m. to 10:30 p.m. in the summer.

Marina Banus

Calle Ramon Areces, 29600

(+34) 952 906 544

http://www.marinabanus.com/

If El Corte Ingles is too overwhelming for you, Marina Banus may be more your style.

Simply head across the road from El Corte Ingles to reach this smaller, budget-friendly mall. Within the mall are approximately 30 stores as well as restaurants and a hair salon. It is also family-friendly with a play area for toddlers. The mall is open Monday through Saturday from 10:00 a.m. to 10:00 p.m. in the winter and daily from 10:30 a.m. to 10:30 p.m. in the summer.

Centro Comercial La Cañada

Carretera Ojén, Marbella 29602

(+34) 95 286 5076

The Centro Comercial La Cañada is similar to Marina Banus in size and has everything you would expect from a mall. The difference is mostly in its ample parking spaces and that it is less crowded than the malls on Puerto Banus. The shops include Armand Basi, Mango, Zara, and Dorothy Perkins and there is a large Alcampo supermarket. The Centro Comercial La Cañada is open daily from 10 a.m. until 10 p.m. (except Sundays).

Zoco del Sol Market

Plaza Antonio Banderas,

Puerto Banus

The Zoco del Sol is an open-air market that occurs daily during the summertime. During the rest of the year, it is open only on Saturdays. Situated on Plaza Antonio Banderas (named after the famous movie actor who was born in the area) between the El Corte Ingles Shopping Center and the port, this market has 25 stalls that sell unique art, vintage clothing, jewelry, fragrances, and glass. Park in the lot under the central square and walk the short distance to the market. It is open from 11 a.m.

MARBELLA TRAVEL GUIDE

until midnight during the summer and from 10 a.m. until 4 p.m. on Saturdays during the rest of the year.

Know Before You Go

 Entry Requirements

By virtue of the Schengen agreement, visitors from other countries in the European Union will not need a visa when visiting Spain. Additionally visitors from Switzerland, Norway, Lichtenstein, Iceland, Canada, the United Kingdom, Australia and the USA are also exempt. Independently travelling minors will need to carry written permission from their parents. If visiting from a country where you require a visa to enter Spain, you will also need to state the purpose of your visit and provide proof that you have financial means to support yourself for the duration of your stay. Unless you are an EU national, your passport should be valid for at least 3 months after the end of your stay.

Health Insurance

Citizens of other EU countries are covered for emergency health care in Spain. UK residents, as well as visitors from Switzerland are covered by the European Health Insurance Card (EHIC), which can be applied for free of charge. Visitors from non-Schengen countries will need to show proof of private health insurance that is valid for the duration of their stay in Spain, as part of their visa application.

🌍 Travelling with Pets

Spain participates in the Pet Travel Scheme (PETS) which allows UK residents to travel with their pets without requiring quarantine upon re-entry. Certain conditions will need to be met. The animal will have to be microchipped and up to date on rabies vaccinations. Additionally, you will need a PETS re-entry certificate issued by a UK vet, an Export Health Certificate (this is required by the Spanish authorities), an official Certificate of Treatment against dangerous parasites such as tapeworm and ticks and an official Declaration that your pet has not left the qualifying countries within this period. Pets from the USA or Canada may be brought in under the conditions of a non-commercial import. For this, your pet will also need to be microchipped (or marked with an identifying tattoo) and up to date on rabies vaccinations.

🌍 Airports

Adolfo Suárez Madrid–Barajas Airport (MAD) is the largest and busiest airport in Spain. It is located about 9km from the financial district of Madrid, the capital. The busiest route is the so-called "Puente Aéreo" or "air bridge", which connects Madrid with Barcelona. The second busiest airport in Spain is **Barcelona–El Prat Airport** (BCN), located about 14km southwest from the center of Barcelona. There are two terminals. The newer Terminal 1 handles the bulk of its traffic, while the older Terminal 2 is used by budget airlines such as EasyJet.

Palma de Mallorca Airport (PMI) is the third largest airport in Spain and one of its busiest in the summer time. It has the capacity of processing 25 million passengers annually. **Gran Canaria Airport** (LPA) handles around 10 million passengers annually and connects travellers with the Canary Islands. **Pablo Ruiz Picasso Malaga Airport** (AGP) provides access to the Costa del Sol. Other southern airports are **Seville Airport** (SVQ), **Jaen Federico Garcia Lorca Airport** (GRX) near Granada, **Jerez de la Frontera Airport**, which connects travellers to Costa del Luz and Cadiz and **Almeria Airport** (LEI).

🌍 Airlines

Iberia is the flag carrying national airline of Spain. Since a merger in 2010 with British Airways, it is part of the International Airlines Group (IAG). Iberia is in partnership with the regional carrier Air Nostrum and Iberia Express, which focusses on medium and short haul routes. Vueling is a low-cost Spanish airline with connections to over 100 destinations. In partnership with MTV, it also provides a seasonal connection to Ibiza. Volotea is a budget airline based in Barcelona, which mainly flies to European destinations. Air Europe, the third largest airline after Iberia and Vueling connects Europe to resorts in the Canaries and the Balearic Islands and also flies to North and South America. Swiftair flies mainly to destinations in Europe, North Africa and the Middle East.

Barcelona-El Prat Airport serves as a primary hub for Iberia Regional. It is also a hub for Vueling. Additionally it functions as a regional hub for Ryanair. Air Europe's primary hubs are at Palma de Mallorca Airport and Madrid Barajas Airport, but other bases are at Barcelona Airport and Tenerife South Airport. Air Nostrum is served by hubs at Barcelona Airport, Madrid Barajas Airport and Valencia Airport. Gran Canaria Airport is the hub for the regional airline, Binter Canarias.

🌐 Currency

Spain's currency is the Euro. It is issued in notes in denominations of €500, €200, €100, €50, €20, €10 and €5. Coins are issued in denominations of €2, €1, 50c, 20c, 10c, 5c, 2c and 1c.

🌐 Banking & ATMs

You should have no trouble making withdrawals in Spain if your ATM card is compatible with the MasterCard/Cirrus or Visa/Plus networks. If you want to save money, avoid using the dynamic currency conversion (DCC) system, which promises to charge you in your own currency for the Euros you withdraw. The fine print is that your rate will be less favorable. Whenever possible, opt to conduct your transaction in Euros instead. Do remember to advise your bank or credit card company of your travel plans before leaving.

🌐 Credit Cards

Visa and MasterCard will be accepted at most outlets that handle credit cards in Spain, but you may find that your American Express card is not as welcome at all establishments. While shops may still be able to accept transactions with older magnetic strip cards, you will need a PIN enabled card for transactions at automatic vendors such as ticket sellers. Do not be offended when asked to show proof of ID when paying by credit card. It is common practice in Spain and Spaniards are required by law to carry identification on them at all times.

MARBELLA TRAVEL GUIDE

🌐 Tourist Taxes

In the region of Catalonia, which includes Barcelona, a tourist tax of between €0.45 and €2.50 per night is levied for the first seven days of your stay. The amount depends on the standard of the establishment, but includes youth hostels, campgrounds, holiday apartments and cruise ships with a stay that exceeds 12 hours.

🌐 Reclaiming VAT

If you are not from the European Union, you can claim back VAT (or Value Added Tax) paid on your purchases in Spain. The VAT rate in Spain is 18 percent. VAT refunds are made on purchases of €90.15 and over from a single shop. Look for shops displaying Global Blue Tax Free Shopping signage. You will be required to fill in a form at the shop, which must then be stamped at the Customs office at the airport. Customs officers will want to inspect your purchases to make sure that they are sealed and unused. Once this is done, you will be able to claim your refund from the Refund Office at the airport. Alternately, you can mail the form to Global Blue once you get home for a refund on your credit card.

🌐 Tipping policy

In general, Spain does not really have much of a tipping culture and the Spanish are not huge tippers themselves. When in a restaurant, check your bill to see whether a gratuity is already included. If not, the acceptable amount will depend on the size of the meal, the prestige of the restaurant and the time of day. For a quick coffee, you can simply round the amount off. For lunch in a modest establishment, opt for 5 percent or one euro per person. The recommended tip for dinner would be more generous, usually somewhere between 7 and 10 percent. This will depend on the type of establishment.

In hotels, if there is someone to help you with your luggage, a tip of 1 euro should be sufficient. At railway stations and airports, a tip is not really expected. Rounding off the amount of the fare to the nearest euro would be sufficient for a taxi driver. If you recruited a private driver, you may wish to tip that person at the end of your association with him.

🌐 Mobile Phones

Most EU countries, including Spain uses the GSM mobile service. This means that most UK phones and some US and Canadian phones and mobile devices will work in Spain. While you could check with your service provider about coverage before you leave, using your own service in roaming mode will involve additional costs. The alternative is to purchase a Spanish SIM card to use during your stay in Spain.

Spain has four mobile networks. They are Movistar, Vodafone, Orange and Yoiga. Buying a Spanish SIM card is relatively simple and inexpensive. By law, you will be required to show some form of identification such as a passport. A basic SIM card from Vodafone costs €5. There are two tourist packages available for €15, which offers a combination of 1Gb data, together with local and international call time. Alternately, a data only package can also be bought for €15. From Orange, you can get a SIM card for free, with a minimum top-up purchase of €10. A tourist SIM with a combination of data and voice calls can be bought for €15. Movistar offers a start-up deal of €10. At their sub-branches, Tuenti, you can also get a free SIM, but the catch is that you need to choose a package to get it. The start-up cost at Yoiga is €20.

Dialling Code

The international dialling code for Spain is +34.

Emergency Numbers

All Emergencies: 112 (no area code required)
Police (municipal): 092
Police (national): 091

MARBELLA TRAVEL GUIDE

Police (tourist police, Madrid): 91 548 85 37

Police (tourist police, Barcelona): 93 290 33 27

Ambulance: 061 or 112

Fire: 080 or 112

Traffic: 900 123 505

Electricity: 900 248 248

Immigration: 900 150 000

MasterCard: 900 958 973

Visa: 900 99 1124

🌐 Public Holidays

1 January: New Year's Day (Año Nuevo)

6 January: Day of the Epiphany/Three Kings Day (Reyes Mago)

March/April: Good Friday

1 May: Labor Day (Día del Trabajo)

15 August: Assumption of Mary (Asunción de la Virgen)

12 October: National Day of Spain/Columbus Day (Fiesta Nacional de España or Día de la Hispanidad)

1 November: All Saints Day (Fiesta de Todos los Santos)

6 December: Spanish Constitution Day (Día de la Constitución)

8 December: Immaculate Conception (La Immaculada)

25 December: Christmas (Navidad)

Easter Monday is celebrated in the Basque region, Castile-La Mancha, Catalonia, La Rioja, Navarra and Valencia. 26

December is celebrated as Saint Stephen's Day in Catalonia and the Balearic Islands.

🌐 Time Zone

Spain falls in the Central European Time Zone. This can be calculated as Greenwich Mean Time/Co-ordinated Universal Time (GMT/UTC) +2; Eastern Standard Time (North America) -6; Pacific Standard Time (North America) -9.

🌐 Daylight Savings Time

Clocks are set forward one hour on the last Sunday in March and set back one hour on the last Sunday in October for Daylight Savings Time.

🌐 School Holidays

Spain's academic year is from mid-September to mid-June. It is divided into three terms with two short breaks of about two weeks around Christmas and Easter.

🌐 Trading Hours

Trading hours in Spain usually run from 9.30am to 1.30pm and from 4.30pm to 8pm, from Mondays to Saturdays. Malls and shopping centers often trade from 10am to 9pm without closing. During the peak holiday seasons, shops could stay open until 10pm. Lunch is usually served between 1pm and 3.30pm while dinner is served from 8.30 to 11pm.

🌐 Driving Laws

The Spanish drive on the right hand side of the road. You will need a driver's licence which is valid in the EC to be able to hire a car in Spain. The legal driving age is 18, but most rental companies will require you to be at least 21 to be able to rent a car. You will need to carry your insurance documentation and rental contract with you at all times, when driving. The speed limit in Spain is 120km per hour on motorways, 100km per hour on dual carriageways and 90km per hour on single carriageways. Bear in mind that it is illegal to drive in Spain wearing sandals or flip-flops.

You may drive a non-Spanish vehicle in Spain provided that it is considered roadworthy in the country where it is registered. As a UK resident, you will be able to drive a vehicle registered in the UK in Spain for up to six months, provided that your liabilities as a UK motorist, such as MOT, road tax and insurance are up to date for the entire period of your stay. The legal limit in Spain is 0.05, but for new drivers who have had their licence for less than two years, it is 0.03.

🌐 Drinking Laws

In Spain, the minimum drinking age is 18. Drinking in public places is forbidden and can be punished with a spot fine. In areas where binge drinking can be a problem, alcohol trading hours are often limited.

🌐 Smoking Laws

In the beginning of 2006, Spain implemented a policy banning smoking from all public and private work places. This includes schools, libraries, museums, stadiums, hospitals, cinemas, theatres and shopping centers as well as public transport. From 2011, smoking was also banned in restaurants and bars, although designated smoking areas can be created provided they are enclosed and well ventilated. Additionally tobacco products may only be sold from tobacconists and bars and restaurants where smoking is permitted. Smoking near children's parks, schools or health centers carries a €600 fine.

🌐 Electricity

Electricity: 220 volts

Frequency: 50 Hz

Your electrical appliances from the UK and Ireland should be able to function sufficiently in Spain, but since Spain uses 2 pin sockets, you will need a C/F adapter to convert the plug from 3 to 2-pins. The voltage and frequency is compatible with UK appliances. If travelling from the USA, you will need a converter or step-down transformer to convert your appliances to 110 volts. The latest models of many laptops, camcorders, cell phones and digital cameras are dual-voltage with a built in converter.

🌍 Food & Drink

Spanish cuisine is heavily influenced by a Moorish past. Staple dishes include the rice dish, Paella, Jamon Serrano (or Spanish ham), Gazpacho (cold tomato-based vegetable soup), roast suckling pig, chorizo (spicy sausage) and the Spanish omelette. Tapas (hot or cold snacks) are served with drinks in Spanish bars.

The most quintessentially Spanish drink is sangria, but a popular alternative with the locals is tinto de verano, or summer wine, a mix of red wine and lemonade. Vino Tinto or red wine compliments most meal choices. The preferred red grape type is Tempranillo, for which the regions of Roija and Ribera del Duero are famous. A well-known sparkling wine, Cava, is grown in Catalonia. Do try the Rebujito, a Seville style mix of sherry, sparkling water and mint. The most popular local beers are Cruzcampo, Alhambra and Estrello Damm. Coffee is also popular with Spaniards, who prefer Café con leche (espresso with milk).

Websites

http://www.idealspain.com

A detailed resource that includes legal information for anyone planning a longer stay or residency in Spain.

http://spainattractions.es/

http://www.tourspain.org/

http://spainguides.com/

http://www.travelinginspain.com/

http://wikitravel.org/en/Spain

Printed in Great Britain
by Amazon